AM I GOOD ENOUGH?

HOW CAN I BE SAVED?

BASIC BIBLE STUDIES ON SALVATION BY GRACE

RICHARD B. RAMSAY

Am I Good Enough? How Can I Be Saved?

Basic Bible Studies on Salvation by Grace

Richard B. Ramsay

ISBN: 979-8-90046-941-6
Staten House

PREFACE

There is a deep need in Christian circles to grasp the importance of *grace*. Many are deprived of the joy that could be theirs because they are still trying to somehow *earn* God's love. They continually ask themselves, "*Am I good enough* to be saved, or to earn God's favor?" I also see a need to comprehend the *full benefits* of our salvation in Christ.

These Bible studies cover some of the most basic doctrines of the Christian faith, focusing on grace. The purpose is to make some very profound biblical doctrines easy to understand.

I would like to thank Erika O'Shee for the line drawings, and especially my wife, Angélica, for encouraging me to write the lessons, and for helping to edit them.

May God's GRACE abound in deepening the faith of many people through the study of these lessons!

Viña del Mar, Chile, 1992

PREFACE TO THE SECOND EDITION IN ENGLISH

Over the last twenty years, I have been amazed at the unusual things the Lord has done with this booklet. For example, it has been translated into Vietnamese, Quechua (Peru and Ecuador), and Bislama (Vanuatu, in the South Pacific), not exactly the languages you might expect! In Peru, a man is using the booklet in a Bible study with people from India! Cuba is experiencing a great revival, and many have used the booklet in home cell groups across the island (*¿Cuán Bueno Debo Ser?* in Spanish). I believe the Lord is making some very unusual cross-cultural connections in our day, and I am overjoyed that this booklet has been a tool for people to come to know Christ and grow in their faith. This has encouraged me to re-edit a second edition in English.

Sue Yarbrough has kindly done some new graphics for the first pages of each chapter. I have also added some introductory readings to each lesson. The rest of the content remains the same.

Miami, 2008

THIRD EDITION

After being distributed by several publishers, for which I am very thankful, this booklet is now being independently published to have more options for accessible distribution, including a *Kindle* version. The content remains basically the same, with some minor modifications, especially in redacting some questions and modifying a few illustrations. The title has also been changed to *Am I Good Enough? How Can I Be Saved?*

Orlando, 2025

The jailer... asked,
"Sirs, what must I do to be saved?"
They replied,
"Believe in the Lord Jesus, and you will be saved—
you and your household."
(Acts 16:29–31)

Is God Like a Light Bulb to You?

"Do you believe in God?", I finally dared to ask my friend, after years of being afraid of his answer. He had never recovered his faith since the class he took in philosophy. The professor declared that he would try to convince us all that God did not exist, and he apparently succeeded with my friend.

"What do you mean? What kind of God?"

"A personal God, you know, one who answers prayers," I explained.

"God has never answered any of my prayers. I have seen just as many answers by praying to the light bulb on the ceiling!"

I would have preferred a dagger in my stomach. It saddened me deeply, because I realized that he didn't know God. Although he had grown up in a Christian family and had attended church twice every Sunday for his whole youth, he didn't have a personal relationship with the Lord.

For many people, God seems far away and impersonal. They feel just as close to a light bulb. How about you?

These lessons will show you that the Bible reveals a God who loves us, relates to us, hears us, speaks to us, and takes care of us. Nothing is more important than developing a personal relationship with God.

CONTENTS

THE AUTHOR

Dr. Ramsay was a missionary in Chile for 21 years, teaching in a seminary and planting churches. There he met his wife, Angelica. They have two adult children, both married. For the last 25 years, they have been traveling to teach conferences and producing resources for theological education. Richard has taught for *Universidad FLET* and *Thirdmill Seminary* and has developed many online courses.

Richard has an M.Div. and a D.Min. from *Westminster Theological Seminary* and a Th.M. from *Covenant Theological Seminary*.

Other books by the author include: *Transformed Into the Image of Jesus, The Certainty of the Faith, Intellectual Integrity, Catholics and Protestants, Basic Greek and Exegesis, Strengthen Your Faith, Synopsis of the Bible, Putting the Pieces Together,* and *Orientation for Leaders.*

BIBLE PASSAGES

You should have a Bible to look up passages (like the *New International Version*, the *English Standard version*, or another version of your choice). Use the index to find the different books of the Bible if necessary. You could also use a Bible software application (such as *e-Sword, Logos, Olive Tree Bible,* or *Bible Gateway*). You should write down answers where you see a blank space or where you see this symbol: ◊◊

1
What is Grace?

WHERE ARE YOU IN THE MANGER SCENE?

The following story from a popular Italian novel represents many peoples' religious experience:

"In the entrance to the school, the sisters had built a large manger scene, which remained standing all year long. There was Jesus in the stable with his father, his mother, an ox and a little donkey, and all around there were mountains and cliffs made of cardboard and rock, where only a flock of little sheep lived. Every one of them represented a student, and depending on his conduct each day, was moved closer or farther away from Jesus.

"Every morning, before going to class, we would pass by the manger, and they made us look to see our position. On the other side of the stable there was a very steep cliff, and that's where the bad girls were put, with two legs suspended over the edge. From six years of age until ten, I lived conditioned by the position of my little sheep. I don't need to tell you that I hardly ever moved from the edge of the cliff."[1]

Is this the way you feel sometimes? If so, there is good news for you! Jesus loves you! He doesn't just push you toward the edge of the cliff and leave you hanging! There is no grace in that perspective! Instead, He goes to bring you back! He is the Good Shepherd who goes out to find the one who is lost and carries him back on His shoulders. God is the Father who receives the prodigal son with open arms and celebrates with a party!

You may sense that you have offended God so often or so severely that there is no hope for you. But please don't

---

[1]Translated by the author from the Spanish version, *Donde el corazón te lleve* [Where Your Heart Leads You] Susana Tamara (Santiago de Chile: Editorial Atlántida, 1995), pp. 66-67.

underestimate the love of God! If you ask Him, He will forgive you. Jesus died on the cross for us! What more could He do to show His love?

Where are you in the manger scene?

FOR PREVIOUS REFLECTION

1. How can you be sure you have eternal life? Do you often imagine God using a balancing scale to weigh your good deeds on one side and your bad deeds on the other? Do you ask yourself if you have been good enough to be saved?

2. How would you define "grace"?

BIBLE STUDY

Read Ephesians 2:8-9.

According to this passage, how can we be saved?

◊◊

Why does God offer salvation as a gift, according to this text?

◊◊

To receive something as a *gift* is to receive it by *grace*. What we want to emphasize in this series of Bible studies is that *God saves us by grace*. That is, we do not *deserve* eternal life, but God *gives* it to us because *He loves us in spite of our sin*.

GRACE IS:
UNMERITED FAVOR

To receive something by grace is the opposite of earning something.

Imagine standing in heaven at the foot of God's throne: How would it seem if someone said, "I'm glad you recognized that I was a good person and let me come to heaven!" or "I knew I was right about Christianity! It's a good thing I was smart enough to realize it was the true religion!"? Both comments betray an

12

arrogant attitude, because the person thinks he did something to *deserve* eternal life.

Your eternal life depends on understanding that salvation is by grace, not by works! You cannot be saved if you think you can somehow *earn* eternal life. The Lord offers salvation as a gift; it can't be purchased!

Imagine that a young man worked hard and saved for several months to be able to give his girlfriend a beautiful diamond engagement ring. How would he feel if she offered to *pay* for it? Imagine how the Lord feels when He has done something much greater for us, and we fail to comprehend the wonder of His love. He sent His Son to obtain our salvation by His death on the cross, and sometimes we still try to pay for it ourselves! Our sin eliminates the possibility of saving ourselves; the requirement is to be perfect! Our best deeds and our most noble intentions can't save us. The only way to obtain eternal life is for the Lord Himself to *give* it to us.

Read Romans 4:1-5.

According to verse three, why was Abraham accepted as righteous before God?

◊◊

What contrast is made in verse four?

◊◊

According to verse five, how can you be considered righteous before God?

◊◊

Which of the following illustrations shows what grace is?

_____ a. A father tells his son that he will buy him a bicycle if he gets good grades in school. The boy makes a big effort and gets the reward.

_____ b. Just before Christmas, a father finds out that his son has received bad grades at school. He is sad about that, but he decides to buy him a bicycle for Christmas anyway, just to show that he loves him. He also begins to help him with his studies.

REVIEW

1. What is "grace?"

◊◊

2. What is the opposite of receiving something by grace?

◊◊

3. Why does God offer salvation by grace?

◊◊

FOR DISCUSSION

1. How does knowing that God loves you by grace, and not by your merits, make you feel? Why?

2. Why do you think some people have a hard time accepting the fact that our salvation is by grace?

TEXT TO MEMORIZE

For it is by grace you have been saved,
through faith--and this not from yourselves,
it is the gift of God--not by works,
so that no one can boast.

(Ephesians 2:8-9)

2
God's Justice and Mercy

JESUS THE RESERVOIR

"The heart of Christ became like a reservoir
in the midst of the mountains.
All the tributary streams of iniquity,
and every drop of the sins of his people,
ran down and gathered into one vast lake,
deep as hell and shoreless as eternity.
All these met, as it were, in Christ's heart,
and he endured them all."
(Charles Spurgeon, 1859)

JESUS THE LIGHTNING ROD

Many tall buildings have iron rods on the roof to protect them against dangerous bolts of lightning. Jesus was our "lightning rod." He received the high voltage of God's wrath against sin and saved us from destruction.

FOR PREVIOUS REFLECTION

When you think about God, how do you picture Him in your mind? Is He smiling? Is He angry? Describe Him.

BIBLE STUDY

There are two incorrect tendencies in the way we think about God: 1. On the one hand, we may imagine Him as being too stern, or 2. On the other hand, we may not take Him seriously enough. In the first case, we fail to understand His mercy, and in the second case, we fail to understand His justice. The Bible teaches us that God is both just and merciful.

Read Romans 1:18.

What makes God angry?

◊◊

Read Romans 2:1.

Why do we have no right to judge others?

◊◊

Read Romans 3:9-20.

How does this passage describe mankind?

◊◊

According to verses 19 and 20, what effect does God's law have on man's heart?

◊◊

Read Matthew 5:22 and John 3:18-19.

What kind of punishment do we deserve for our sin?

◊◊

Do you believe that you would have to suffer eternal condemnation if it weren't for Jesus?

◊◊

Read Romans 3:21-26.

In verse 25, Jesus is called a "propitiation." (The *New International Version* uses the phrase, "a sacrifice of atonement.") This comes from a very special word used in the Old Testament, before Christ. Israel had a temple where God manifested His presence. The outer room was called the "Holy Place," and the back room was called the "Holiest of Holies." The *ark of the covenant* was kept in the "Holiest of Holies." It was a wooden box with a copy of God's Law inside, and it had a golden covering on top called the "atonement cover," or the "mercy seat." Two golden figures of angels called "cherubim" sat on top. Once a year the high priest entered the Holiest of Holies to sprinkle the blood of a sacrificed lamb over this "atonement cover" (Exodus 25:10-22). The act signified the washing away of the sins of God's people, or the "propitiation." The killing of the lamb represented a substitute sacrifice that calmed the wrath of God. This was a symbol of Jesus, the "Lamb of God" they were looking forward to, whose blood covers our sins.

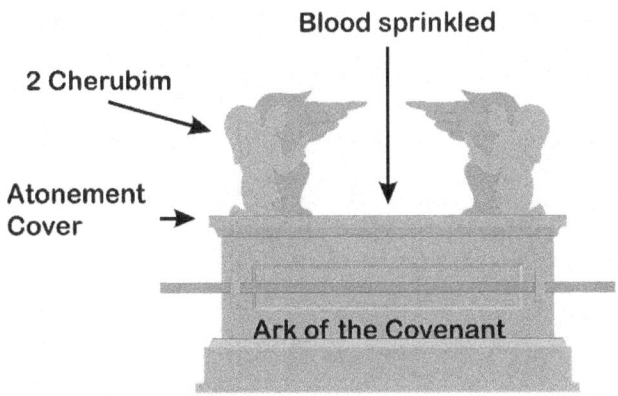

Blood sprinkled

2 Cherubim

Atonement Cover

Ark of the Covenant

A "*PROPITIATION*" (*OR A "SACRIFICE OF ATONEMENT*") IS A:

SACRIFICE WHICH TAKES AWAY THE WRATH OF GOD.

In Romans 3:21-26, Paul teaches us that this is the way God manifests both His justice and His mercy at the same time. Think about this: If God simply overlooked sin, He wouldn't be just; however, if He chose just to pour out His wrath on mankind, He wouldn't be merciful. Thus, when He sent Jesus to be punished for our sin, He carried out justice, but He also mercifully provided us an escape from eternal condemnation.

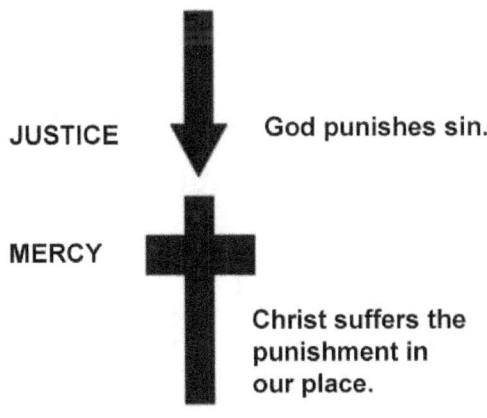

JUSTICE — God punishes sin.

MERCY

Christ suffers the punishment in our place.

How does God show His justice and mercy on the cross?

◊◊

Jesus is called a P_____ (or "Sacrifice of A _____.")

REVIEW

1. In this lesson we studied two aspects of God's character:

   His J _____ and His M _____.

2. How does Romans 3 describe mankind?

◊◊

3. What do we all deserve because of our sin?

◊◊

4. How does God demonstrate His justice and His mercy at the same time?

◊◊

5. What is a "propitiation" or a "sacrifice of atonement"?

◊◊

For Discussion

1. Has your concept of God changed in any way after studying this lesson? How?

2. What are some practical implications of the fact that God is both just and merciful at the same time? Think of how this should affect your relationship with other people.

Text to Memorize

But because of His great love for us, God, who is rich in mercy, made us alive with Christ while we were dead in transgressions -- it is by grace you have been saved.

(Ephesians 2:4-5)

3
The Creation;
Everything in Harmony

BETTER THAN YOUR FAVORITE PLACE

One of my favorite places is Southern Chile. There are snow-covered volcanoes, lively streams, beautiful lakes, rich green hills, and the happiest cows in the world! When I go there, my mind and spirit are totally renewed. I forget all my problems, relax before the peaceful scenery, and enjoy the irresistible pastries, coffee, sandwiches, and chocolates.

It gives me a small taste of what the Garden of Eden must have been like at first! You probably have a favorite place too. But Eden was more wonderful than anything we can experience now, because sin had not yet brought corruption into the world. Everything was still in harmony, and most important of all, they had a close relationship with God and with each other.

Imagine what the Garden of Eden was like for Adam and Eve. What kind of relationship did they have with each other? With the animals? With God?

BIBLE STUDY

The world at times seems full of conflict: war, sickness, hunger, tragedy, and all kinds of suffering. Some people blame God and ask why He allows it to happen. In this lesson, we will see that in the beginning God made everything in perfect harmony.

Read Genesis 1:1-2:3.

Name some of the things God created on each day.

◊◊

What phrase is repeated in the following verses? 1:4, 1:12, 1:18, 1:21, 1:25, and 1:31

◊◊

This indicates that everything God made was good, and that in the beginning there was no conflict in the creation.

27

From the creation account we can see that:

a. God is good, because He made everything good.
b. God is a personal God. He talks, he reasons, he has emotions, and he appreciates beauty.
c. God is powerful. He made all things just by speaking.

What else can you learn about God in this passage? Write down your ideas.

◊◊

The fact that God is a personal God implies that:

a. We can communicate with Him.
b. We can love Him and be loved by Him.
c. He has emotions; He can be happy, sad, angry, joyful.
d. He is creative and appreciates beauty.

Can you think of some other implications? Write down your ideas.

◊◊

We can also learn some important things about human beings in the account of the creation:

a. We are the image of God.
b. We are male and female.
c. We were given authority over the earth and the animals.

What else can you learn about mankind in this passage? Write down your ideas.

◊◊

TO SAY THAT WE ARE *THE IMAGE OF GOD* BASICALLY MEANS WE ARE:

> **SIMILAR TO GOD, BUT NOT EQUAL.**

This means, for example, that we also:

a. are creative.
b. have emotions.
c. reason and make decisions.
d. have a sense of humor.
e. have a sense of right and wrong.
f. use language to communicate.
g. appreciate beauty.

Can you think of other aspects of the image of God? Think, for example, of things that make us different from animals.

◊◊

REVIEW

1. The main point of this lesson is that God made everything in

   H _____.

2. God saw that everything was G_____.

3. We emphasized one aspect of God, that He is a P_____ God.

4. We emphasized one aspect of human beings, that we are the I_____ of God.

5. This basically means that we are _____.

FOR DISCUSSION

1. After the Fall, are human beings still the image of God? (see Genesis 9:6)

2. How does it affect your attitude toward other people to know that they are made in the image of God? Does it change the way you relate to people that seem hard to respect? Can you give an example?

3. Can the biblical story of the creation be reconciled with the theory of evolution? How? What is your opinion?

TEXT TO MEMORIZE

God saw all that He had made, and it was very good....

(Genesis 1:31)

4
The Fall; Separation

Worse Than an Atomic Bomb

The Fall of mankind was worse than an atomic bomb; sin blew all relationships into pieces and corrupted everything. Conflict now dominates the creation. We have all become self-centered. We ache to regain the sense that existed before the Fall of wholeness, of belonging, and of being loved. We long to return to the Garden of Eden, but the gate is closed.

Some people try to explain away human guilt, saying that it is just the influence of society that makes us feel guilty. However, the Bible teaches that there is true guilt. Although sometimes we feel guilty unnecessarily, often we have actually done something wrong. When we sin, we not only have a guilty *conscience*, but we also have a *guilty record* in God's sight, for which we deserve punishment.

We underestimate the gravity of our sin. The problem is not that we do something wrong in the abstract; the problem is that we personally offend a holy God every time we sin in our words, our thoughts, our feelings, and our deeds. Furthermore, we also sin when we don't do things that we should do.

Remember that He is the all-powerful, all-knowing creator of the universe. If we came face to face with Him, we would tremble and bow before Him.

[Previous picture is from a painting by Hennyer E. Delgado Chacón]

Imagine yourself in the place of Adam and Eve after the Fall:

1. How were things different from their life before the Fall?

2. How did sin affect humanity and the world?

3. How did they feel after God expelled them from the Garden of Eden?

BIBLE STUDY

We can't blame God for the problems in the world, because God made everything good. Human beings caused the problems when they sinned. In this lesson, we will analyze the results of the Fall.

Read Genesis 2:16-17.

What was the only prohibition in the Garden of Eden?

◊◊

Read Genesis 3:1.

How did the serpent distort this commandment?

◊◊

Read Genesis 3:4-5.

What motive did the serpent say that God had in giving this commandment?

◊◊

Read Genesis 3:6.

Why did Eve decide to eat the fruit?

◊◊

What can we learn about the nature of temptation in this passage? Write down your thoughts.

◊◊

Adam and Eve decided to listen to the serpent instead of God. Basically, the Fall was an attempt to become independent of God. When God told them not to eat the fruit, that they would die if they ate it, they should have believed Him simply because it was God their creator who said it. Nevertheless, they doubted Him and made a decision based on what they thought was correct. They pretended to know more than God in that moment; they put themselves above Him and became rulers over their own lives. In a word, the root cause of the Fall was arrogance.

Let's analyze the results of sin, reviewing chapter 3 of Genesis.

What consequences of the Fall are shown in the following verses?

a. Vs. 7.

◊◊

b. Vv. 8-10.

◊◊

c. Vv. 12-13.

◊◊

d. Vs. 16.

◊◊

e. Vv. 17-18.

◊◊

f. Vs. 19.

◊◊

g. Vv. 23-24.

◊◊

Which of the following relationships were broken as a result of sin?

___ a. Between people and God.

___ b. Between people and other people.

___ c. Between people and nature.

___ d. Between people and their own hearts.

Read Romans 5:12.

How did Adam's sin affect the world?

S____ and D_____ spread throughout the whole world.

The following drawing illustrates the results of the Fall:

REVIEW

1. The Fall was an attempt to become I_____ of God.

2. The root cause of the Fall was an attitude of A_____.

3. As a result of the Fall, the relationships were broken between:

    a. People and _____.
    b. People and _____.
    c. People and _____.
    d. People and _____.

4. Through the sin of Adam, S_____ and D_____ spread through the whole world.

FOR DISCUSSION

In what concrete ways do you see the results of the Fall studied in this lesson most obviously manifest in society today?

TEXT TO MEMORIZE

Therefore, just as sin came into the world through one man,
and death through sin, and so death spread to all men
because all sinned.
(Romans 5:12)

36

5
The Work of Christ; Reconciliation

What if God Were One of Us?

A song that was popular a few years ago speculates about God:

"What if God was one of us? Just a slob like one of us?
Just a stranger on the bus, trying to make his way home?"
(Joan Osborne, "One of Us")

Although this song is irreverent, it does pose an interesting question. What if God were one of us, living a somewhat normal life among us? Would we be able to look Him in the face and talk to Him? What would it be like around Him?

It sounds absurd at first, but this is what God already did in the person of Jesus! It would be very offensive to call Him a "slob," but He did have a name, and people did walk around with Him, look Him in the face, and talk to Him. Isn't that amazing? God in human flesh!

He Gave His Life for Us

The first death that I remember was that of Mr. Hanlon, our neighbor and the father of one of my best friends. Mr. Hanlon was our Cub Scout leader who often took us camping, fishing, and swimming near our hometown, Dodge City, Kansas. I still remember when we got the phone call, telling us that Mr. Hanlon had drowned in the Arkansas river. The river wasn't more than a stream, but it had some whirlpools that could be dangerous. My friend Bill and his sister Wilma were caught in a current and couldn't get out. Their dad jumped in and pulled one out, then the other. In the process, he lost his strength and couldn't resist. He was pulled under and never came back up. This is what Jesus did for us. He gave His life to save us.

But there are two differences: First, Jesus purposefully laid down His life for us. It wasn't an accident. Secondly, He overcame death and Satan and rose again victoriously.

Jesus once asked the disciples, "Who do people say that the Son of Man is?" They answered that some were saying He was John the Baptist, Elijah, Jeremiah, or one of the prophets. Then Jesus turned the question around to them: "Who do *you* say that I am?" (Matthew 16:13-15). Is there a more important question? Who do *you* think Jesus is?

"I believe that there is nothing more beautiful,
more profound, more compassionate, more reasonable,
more valuable and more perfect than Christ."
(Fyodor Dostoyesvsky)

What does "salvation" mean in the Bible?

BIBLE STUDY

Sometimes we talk about being "saved" as if it only meant going to heaven when we die. While it is true that this is one of the most wonderful promises in the gospel, the Bible teaches that our salvation includes many other blessings as well.

Read Colossians 1:18-20.

According to verse 20, what was God's purpose in sending Jesus to die on the cross?

◊◊

In verse 18, what does the phrase "firstborn from the dead" suggest? What happened three days after Jesus' crucifixion?

◊◊

What are the two important events in Jesus' redemptive work mentioned in these verses?

His D_____ and His R_____.

How would you define "salvation," according to these verses?

◊◊

Read Ephesians 1:10.

According to this verse, what was God's intention in sending Christ?

◊◊

How would you explain the concept of "salvation," according to this verse?

◊◊

In both passages, there is a key phrase that describes the work of Christ.

   In Colossians 1:20 the word is *"reconcile."*
   In Ephesians 1:10 the phrase is *"bring together" (or "unite").*

How many things have been "reconciled" or "brought together" in Christ, according to these verses?

◊◊

What are the implications? Which of these relationships are included in our reconciliation?

____ a. With God
____ b. With other people
____ c. With nature
____ d. With ourselves

We will give two definitions of "salvation":

THE FIRST DEFINITION OF **SALVATION**:

THE RECONCILIATION OF ALL THINGS IN CHRIST

Jesus came to reconcile God and man, suffering for our sins, nailing our debt to the cross, and rose again victorious over the power of sin and death. This reconciliation with God carries over into other dimensions of our lives. Once we are right with God, this affects our relationships with other people, with nature itself, and with ourselves.

Christ undoes all the effects of the Fall. All the conflicts produced by sin are healed in Christ. We are freed from their damage. This gives us the second definition of salvation:

THE SECOND DEFINITION OF **SALVATION**:

LIBERATION FROM SIN AND ALL ITS CONSEQUENCES

Consider the results of the Fall and write down some specific problems which will eventually be cured because of what Jesus did for us:

Think of your family:

◊◊

Think of your emotions:

◊◊

42

Think of your intellect:

◊◊

Think of your eternal life:

◊◊

Think of your physical body:

◊◊

Think of your integrity and character:

◊◊

Think of your work:

◊◊

Think of other areas of your life:

◊◊

Read Philippians 3:12.

What does this verse tell us about when we experience all the aspects of our salvation?

◊◊

The salvation that Christ purchased for us is **total**. However, we don't receive all the benefits right away. Our salvation will be completed only when Jesus returns and establishes the eternal form of His kingdom. Our salvation has been **won**, but it has not been **finished** yet.

It's like inheriting millions of dollars which are invested in a savings account. The money is already in your name, but you don't receive it all at once. You receive regular dividends, but you have to wait until the appropriate time to receive the full amount. We receive continual blessings of our salvation, but we will not see the full benefits until Jesus returns.

Observe the following diagram:

THE OVERLAPPING AGES

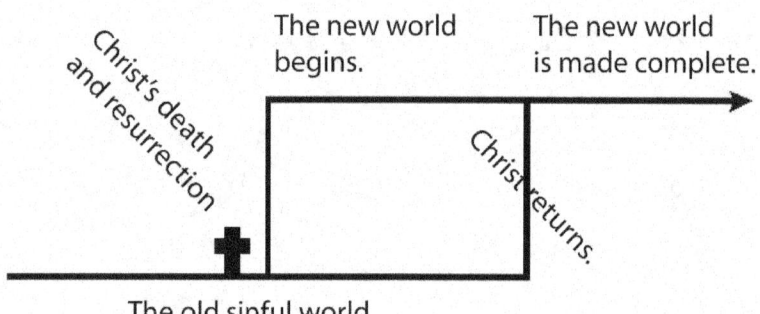

When Jesus died and rose again, the new era began. Nevertheless, the old sinful age does not end until Jesus returns. In the meantime, we live in the period of transition (or overlap) between the two ages. Jesus already purchased our salvation, but we don't experience all the benefits until He sets up His kingdom in final form.

If you believe in Jesus as Lord and Savior, you are already reconciled with God, and the process of liberation from sin and its damage is in progress. During the transition period, there are three categories to describe the different aspects of salvation:

1. *Already,*
2. *Not Yet, and*

3. In Process.

Try to identify the aspects which are already done for you ("Already"), the ones which have not yet begun ("Not Yet"), and the ones which have begun, but are not yet finished ("In Process").

a. _____ Your sins are forgiven.

b. _____ You are a child of God, adopted forever.

c. _____ You have a new body.

d. _____ You will not die a physical death.

e. _____ There is a new heaven and a new earth.

f. _____ You love your neighbor.

g. _____ You understand the truth.

h. _____ You live justly.

REVIEW

1. What did Jesus do to obtain our salvation?

◊◊

2. Write the two definitions of salvation explained in this lesson.

◊◊

3. Our salvation has been W____, but it is not yet F_____.

For Discussion

1. Have you been reconciled with God? That is, have you asked for forgiveness for your sins, trusting Jesus for your salvation?

If you haven't done that yet, you can do it now, simply by praying. You can ask God to forgive you for all your sins, even the ones you are not conscious of or don't remember, and thank Him for the pardon that Jesus already has gained for you on the cross.

2. What practical implications do you see in the two definitions of "salvation"?

3. What do you think of the diagram of "The Overlapping Ages"? Does it make sense to you? Do you have questions? Is it helpful for you?

4. If you have been reconciled with God, do you see the fruit of your new relationship with God reflected in your relationship with other people? How should this be shown?

Text to Memorize

And through him to reconcile to himself all things, whether things on earth or things in heaven, by making peace through his blood, shed on the cross.

(Colossians 1:20)

6
The Call

"Come and follow me!"

A friend of mine had been a hippie when he was a young man. He had gone to live in a commune in California. Eventually he traveled around the world looking for the meaning of life.

When he felt betrayed by some friends, he returned to the United States. One day, he was browsing around in the basement of his grandfather's house, and he picked up a small New Testament. He began to read it and couldn't put it down. He said, "When I finished reading the gospels, I realized who Jesus was. I knew that when He said, 'Come and follow me, I had no choice!'"

How about you? Have you realized who Jesus is? Have you sensed Him saying to you, "Come and follow me"?

Have you answered His call?

When did the process of your salvation begin?

BIBLE STUDY

One of the Bible teachings that gives us most comfort and security is the fact that it is God who takes the initiative in our salvation. He began it and He will finish it.

Read Ephesians 1:3-5.

According to this passage, when did God choose us?

◊◊

Read 1 John 4:19.

Who took the initiative in loving first?

◊◊

Read Romans 8:29-30.

Before calling us, God did two things. What are they?

    a._____

    b._____

Notice that it does NOT say God foreknew something *about* these people. It literally says that He *knew* the *people* themselves personally beforehand. It means that God *loved* us in eternity before we were born! There is an important difference between knowing things *about* Napoleon and knowing *him* personally.

This passage is parallel to Ephesians 1:3-5 that we read above, where Paul says God "chose us in him before the foundation of the world, that we should be holy and blameless before him. In love he predestined us for adoption to himself as sons." That's when our salvation began! He who is above time loved us from before the creation of the world! This eternal love is the reason He chose us to become like Jesus, and it's the reason He sent Jesus to die for us! How wonderful and comforting to know this!

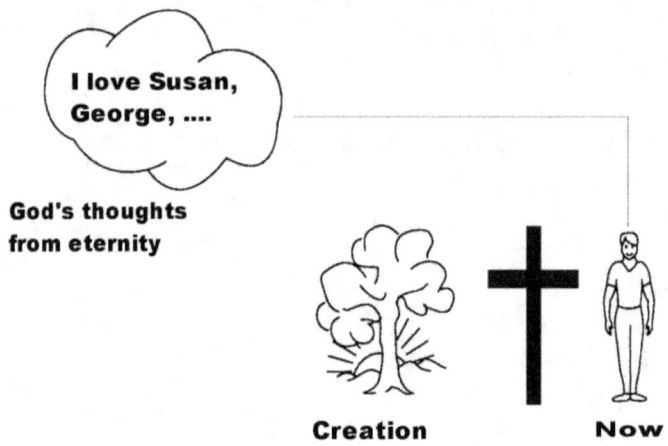

The word "predestine" means to *plan beforehand.*

According to Romans 8:29, what did God predestine with regard to those that He foreknew?

◊◊

GOD:
  1. **KNEW US (LOVED US),**
  2. **PREDESTINED US,**
  3. **CALLED US.**

God did not call us because we were "good" people, because we had faith, because He knew we were going to believe, because

50

we went to church, or because we belonged to a Christian family. Any of these reasons would mean something in *us* is the basis for our salvation. On the contrary, God chose us only because of His loving *GRACE*.

DEFINITION OF THE *CALL*:

There are two theological meanings of the word:

a. The exterior call:

  GOS CAUSES US TO HEAR THE GOSPEL

b. The interior call:

  GOD BRINGS US TO CHRIST, RENEWING OUR HEARTS SO THAT WE BELIEVE IN HIM

Read Romans 10:13-15.

Notice the steps in the process of how God works in our lives to bring us to salvation. To be saved, we must believe and call on the Lord, asking Him to save us.

And before we can believe, what must happen?

◊◊

God, in His perfect plan, normally uses human messengers to bring the gospel to us. These might be friends or family, a pastor or a colleague. He might also lead people to write books, produce movies, or a preach a sermon on TV.

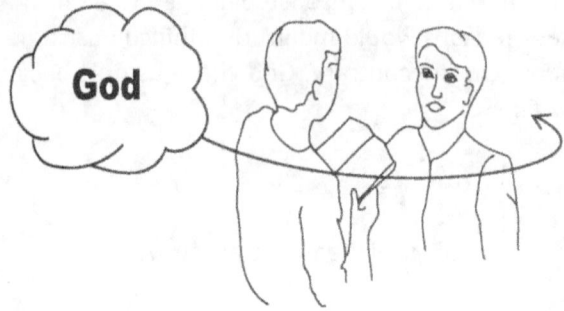

Read Matthew 22:14.

Not everyone who receives the *external* call is saved. For that, we need to believe in Jesus. And to believe in Him, we need to be called *internally*.

Read John 3:3.

To see the kingdom of God, you must be _____.

Being *born again* is an important aspect of the *internal call*. The theological term for this is "*regeneration*." It means that the Holy Spirit gives us a new heart capable of responding to the gospel in faith.

This is the order:

> God loves us.
> God predestines us.
> God calls us externally.
> God calls us internally.

As we will explain more fully in the next chapters, we must respond with repentance and faith.

Read Acts 16:29–31.

What do Paul and Silas tell the Philippian jailer he must do to be saved?

◊◊

REVIEW

1. Write the two definitions:

a. External call:

◊◊

b. Internal call:

◊◊

2. When did the process of your salvation begin?

◊◊

3. Write these terms in their proper order: external call, internal call, predestination, God's love

53

a. _____

b. _____

c. _____

d. _____

4. What does *predestine* mean?

◊◊

5. What is another word for being born again?

◊◊

FOR DISCUSSION

1. Does the fact that God has chosen us from before the foundation of the world mean that we are totally passive in the process of receiving our salvation? What must we do?

2. Before studying this lesson, did you know that God loved you and chose you from before the foundation of the world? How does it make you feel? Does it make you more certain of your salvation?

TEXT TO MEMORIZE

For He chose us in him before the foundation of the world
to be holy and blameless in his sight.

(Ephesians 1:4)

7
Repentance

"OUT, DAMNED SPOT!"

In Shakespeare's play, Lady Macbeth had urged her husband to commit murder, and she eventually went insane, due to her sense of guilt. She imagines her hands to be permanently stained with blood and rubs her hands desperately to remove it. She cries, "Out, damned spot!" But she can't eliminate her guilt.

Only true repentance can bring forgiveness and peace of heart.

SALTY COFFEE

I remember sitting on the balcony of an apartment in Cuba, having breakfast with the director of the *Los Pinos* Seminary. His wife served us each a cup of Cuban expresso, with that unmistakable aroma, and offered what looked like a bowl of sugar. Ramón and I both enthusiastically tossed two spoonfuls of the white powder into our coffee and stirred it up. Before I put the cup to my mouth, Ramón took a sip, wrinkled his face and shouted, "Margarita, this is salt, not sugar!" Margarita turned red and apologized over and over, "I'm so sorry! I'm so sorry!" What could she do? Only one thing: She had to bring fresh coffee. No matter how much sugar you add, it still won't taste good. That's the way sin affects our lives; you can't simply add good works to make the flavor of guilt go away. The damage is done. We need to be renewed spiritually.

Only true repentance can bring spiritual renewal.

What is "repentance"?

BIBLE STUDY

Read Acts 17:30.

What are all people commanded to do?

◊◊

Read Acts 3:19.

What happens to our sins when we repent?

◊◊

Read 2 Corinthians 7:9-10.

What attitude is related to true repentance?

◊◊

Read Luke 3:8 and Acts 26:20.

What else does true repentance include, according to these verses?

◊◊

DEFINITION:

REPENTANCE IS...

To repent is to make a full turn. You have been walking in the path of sin, and you turn away from it to Jesus.

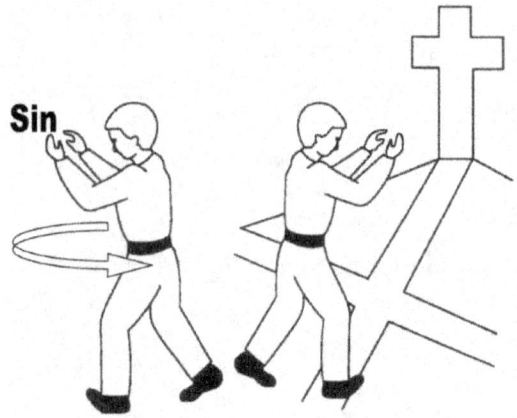

Repentance includes:

    a. feeling sadness for your sin,
    b. asking forgiveness,
    c. abandoning the sin, and
    d. following Jesus.

Which of the following people has truly repented?

_____ a. "I am tired of getting drunk and getting into fights! I always end up in The hospital! I'm going to change my life!"

_____ b. "I feel very bad about having offended you, Lord. I've been dishonest and self-centered. Forgive me and help me to change."

_____ c. "I know that I should stop taking money from the cash register, but I can always go to church on Sunday and confess my sins."

Explain what is wrong in the two cases above where the repentance was not real:

◊◊

Read Mark 10:17-22.

Was the rich young man truly repentant?

◊◊

What would have made his repentance valid?

◊◊

Read Luke 15:17-21.

How does the prodigal son show true repentance?

◊◊

Read Psalm 51:1-10.

What can we learn about true repentance from this Psalm?

◊◊

Read John 13:10.

There is a *first repentance* which is the first step in becoming a Christian and starting a new life. It is like washing your whole body.

However, after the first cleansing, we still continue to sin, and we need to repent frequently. This is like washing our feet.

The first repentance is for salvation, and the other repentances are for continual forgiveness.

1. Define repentance.

◊◊

2. Explain the difference between the first main repentance and other frequent experiences of repentance.

◊◊

FOR PERSONAL REFLECTION

1. Have you experienced true repentance in the first sense of the word? That is, have you felt sorry for your sin and asked the Lord to forgive you and let you start a new life? If not, you should do that now! Don't let another day go by without considering your sins and asking for His cleansing. You can begin a new life, walking in His paths. He will not disappoint you!

2. If you have already made that decision, and are following Jesus, do you have a regular habit of reflecting on your sins and asking forgiveness?

FOR DISCUSSION

1. Analyze this comment from a movie. Does it seem correct? Why, or why not?

"Love means never having to say you're sorry."

2. What is the difference between true repentance and a "New Year's resolution"?

...Now he commands all people everywhere to repent.

(Acts 17:30b)

8
Saving Faith

Saving Faith is Not a "Blind Leap"

Some theologians consider Christian faith an absurd act of the will, against all reason. According to them, there is no reason to believe, but we do anyway. Francis Schaeffer corrected this misunderstanding, insisting that there was a difference between true Christian faith and an existential blind leap. The following is a summary of his illustration:

Imagine that some mountain climbers are lost in the alps when a cold fog settles in. Their guide says they will freeze to death by morning unless they find shelter. He takes them into a dense fog to keep warm, but he has no idea where they are. One of the climbers decides to use his rope and desperately drops down off a cliff, hoping to possibly find a place to protect himself from the cold. This would be a blind leap of faith, not exactly a wise decision.

Now suppose that the others hear the voice of man telling them he knows where a ledge is that would shelter them. They ask who he is and realize that his name is of a well-known family from the area. They ask other questions, and as he continues to give them clear and convincing answers, they begin to trust him. Finally, they drop over where he has indicated, they find refuge and survive.

This is Christian faith, informed and certain, based on a personal relationship of trust, and not a blind leap.

[Francis Schaeffer, *He is There and He is Not Silent* (Wheaton: Tyndale, 1980), appendix.]

What does it mean to "believe" in Jesus?

BIBLE STUDY

In the previous lesson, we explained that when someone repents, he abandons his sin and follows Jesus. But to follow Jesus one needs *faith*. In this lesson, we will study what it means to *believe* in Jesus. There are different kinds of faith, but only one that leads us to salvation. First, we will look at what saving faith *is not*, then at what it *is*.

I. WHAT SAVING FAITH IS NOT

A. Saving faith is not mere intellectual knowledge.

Someone might think, "I believe in Jesus," meaning that he knows that a man named Jesus really existed. It's just like saying he believes in *Napoleon*.

Read James 2:19.

What correct thing do the demons believe?

◊◊

Do you think the demons are saved because of this?

◊◊

People can believe many correct things about God without having saving faith. Of course, sound intellectual knowledge is good and necessary, but it is not *sufficient* to be saved.

◊◊

B. Saving faith is not simply faith in miracles.

Other people think they have a lot of faith because they believe that God does miracles. Maybe they have been healed or seen some other unusual manifestation of God's power.

Read John 3:1-3.

Did Nicodemus believe that Jesus had done miracles?

◊◊

Was he saved because of believing that?

◊◊

What did he need before he could have saving faith?

◊◊

Read 2 Thessalonians 2:9-11.

Who else can perform miracles (counterfeit)?

It is good to believe in God's power to perform miracles, but it is not *sufficient* in order to be saved. Even Satan believes God can do miracles, in fact he does them himself in order to deceive people!

C. Saving faith is not an uncertain hope.

Some people say that faith is "believing the impossible." They think, "If I could be sure, then I wouldn't need faith." But this can be a way of covering up real uncertainty. Maybe they *hope*, for example, that Jesus rose from the dead, but they really aren't sure. What they really have is not *faith*, but an *uncertain hope*. The concept of a "blind leap" is an expression of uncertain hope.

Read Hebrews 11:1.

Write this statement about faith in your own words.

◊◊

II. WHAT SAVING FAITH IS.

SAVING FAITH IS:

> **TRUSTING JESUS AS LORD AND SAVIOR**

It is a personal relationship with Jesus, in which you trust Him for your salvation and submit your life to Him.

A. Jesus is Savior

Read 1 Corinthians 15:1-8.

According to this passage, one must believe the gospel to be saved.

According to verses 3 and 8, what are the essential doctrines of the gospel?

a. That Christ _____

b. That Christ _____

c. That Christ _____

d. That Christ_____

To say that we must believe that Jesus died for our sins is to say that we should trust Jesus as our S_____.

*Some people say that they believe Jesus died for the sins of the world, but they have not personally received His forgiveness for their **own** sins. **Have you accepted His forgiveness?** If you have not done it, you can confess your sins directly to Him in prayer, and He will forgive you.*

Read 1 John 1:9.

If you asked His forgiveness, are your sins forgiven?

◊◊

Are there any sins which remain unforgiven?

◊◊

Read Romans 6:14.

Sin shall not be our _____.

Jesus not only frees us from the *guilt* of sin, but also from the *power* of sin. He *forgives* us and he *frees* us.

B. Jesus is Lord

Read Luke 9:23-25.

To be saved, what must you do, according to this text?

◊◊

Read Romans 10:9-11.

To be saved, what must you confess with your mouth?

◊◊

What must you believe in your heart?

◊◊

These two passages indicate that we should trust in Jesus as
_____.

Perhaps you know that Jesus is "Lord," but you have not
personally submitted your life to Him. If not, you can turn your
life over to Him by praying, asking Him to guide you and telling
Him that you desire to live according to His will.

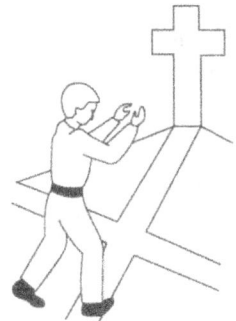

Read Matthew 1:21-23.

Write down the two names of the child, and the meaning of each
one:

◊◊

Write the name that suggests that we should trust in Jesus...

    as Lord: _____

    as Savior: _____

69

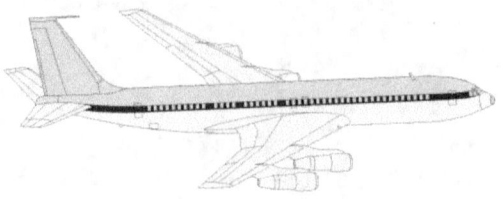

Having faith in Jesus is like having faith in an airplane. You can know many things about an airplane without personally trusting it. People might say they trust a plane, but the only way to know whether they really trust it is if they are willing to board the plane for a flight! It's like that with Jesus. Some people think they have faith in Him, but they've never "boarded the plane." They only have intellectual faith. Perhaps they believe He existed, that he was a good man, they may even believe he died for the sins of the world. However, it's not personal. They haven't accepted forgiveness for their own sins and haven't handed over control of their lives to Him.

How about you?
Are you trusting Jesus in that sense?
Have you "boarded the plane?"

The most important decision in your life is this: *Am I going to accept Jesus Christ as Lord and Savior in my life?* Do it today! Receive His forgiveness and turn your life over to Him!

REVIEW

1. Explain three things that saving faith *is not:*

◊◊

2. Explain what saving faith *is:*

◊◊

FOR DISCUSSION

1. Is it possible that someone might be mistaken about some of the doctrines he believes and still be saved? What are some basic doctrines that one must believe to be saved?

2. What does it mean practically in our daily lives to accept Jesus as Lord?

TEXT TO MEMORIZE

That if you confess with your mouth, "Jesus is Lord,"
and believe in your heart that God raised him from the dead,
you will be saved.

(Romans 10:9)

9
Justification

STANDING ON THE GALLOWS WITH MY HEAD IN A NOOSE

In his senior years, Bob Dylan sings of his fear of condemnation.

> I'm well dressed, waiting on the last train,
> Standing on the gallows with my head in a noose.
> Any minute now I'm expecting all hell to break loose.
> I've been walking forty miles of bad road.
> If the Bible is right, the world will explode.
> I've been trying to get as far away from myself as I can.

(*Things Have Changed*, 2000)

How about you? Do you have peace with God? Or do you still sense a black cloud between you and God?

How would you explain what "justification" means?

BIBLE STUDY

Man has always asked himself, "How can I be considered righteous before God?" (See Job 25:4 and 9:2, for example.) When you think about God the creator, holy and perfect, you don't feel very righteous. You feel guilty and seek peace in your heart. Sometimes people look for this peace in the wrong way, maybe trying to do "good deeds," or maybe submitting themselves to suffering to somehow expiate for their sins. In this lesson, we will explain the only way to be considered righteous by God.

Read Romans 5:18-19.

When Adam sinned, how did this affect mankind's legal standing before God?

    a. It resulted in C _____ for all men. (vs. 18)

    b. People were made S _____. (vs. 19)

What did Jesus' righteousness bring?

    a. It resulted in J _____. (vs. 18)

    b. People will be made R _____. (vs. 19)

DEFINITION:

JUSTIFICATION IS...

> **A DIVINE VERDICT**
> **SAYING WE ARE RIGHTEOUS AND NOT GUILTY.**

An easy way to remember this is to say that when I'm *justified* it's:

> *JUST AS IF I'D NEVER SINNED*

The **BASIS** of our justification is the **WORK OF CHRIST**, not good conduct or human merit of any kind.

Justification does not mean "justifying yourself," giving false excuses, neither does it mean that we actually become totally righteous in our conduct. Justification is our *legal standing* before God. We are *declared* just.

This has two aspects:

a. Our sins are forgiven (past, present and future!)

b. Jesus' perfect righteousness is put on our account.

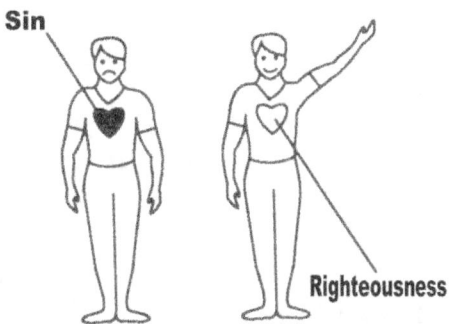

Read Romans 3:9-20.

Sum up in one phrase the main point of this passage.

◊◊

Read Romans 3:21-31.

Sum up the main point of this section.

◊◊

How are we justified according to verse 24?

◊◊

Why do you think God wanted justification to be by faith? (See verses 26 and 27.)

◊◊

According to the conclusion in verse 28, man is justified by F_____ apart from observing the L ____.

Read Romans 4:2-3.

Abraham B_____ God and it was credited to him as righteousness.

Read Romans 4:16.

Why does the promise of blessing come by faith?

◊◊

Read Romans 4:10-11.

Was Abraham justified *before* or *after* being circumcised?

◊◊

Then could Abraham say that he had already been justified at the point in time when he was circumcised, or did he have to wait until he died to be sure if he was justified?

◊◊

Following the same argument, is it arrogant to say that you have already been justified and are already saved, if you believe in Jesus?

◊◊

Read Romans 5:1.

What is the result of being justified?

◊◊

a. The *DEFINITION* of *JUSTIFICATION* is: **A DIVINE VERDICT SAYING WE ARE RIGHTEOUS AND NOT GUILTY.**

b. The *BASIS* of our justification is: **THE WORK OF CHRIST.**

c. The *MEANS* of being justified is: **FAITH.**

d. The *RESULT* of being justified is: **PEACE WITH GOD.**

Faith is like an open hand that reaches out to receive a gift.

Justification is as if you were a murderer condemned to death, and Jesus offered to die in your place. God the Father is the judge, and He accepts Jesus' offer, declaring you not guilty.

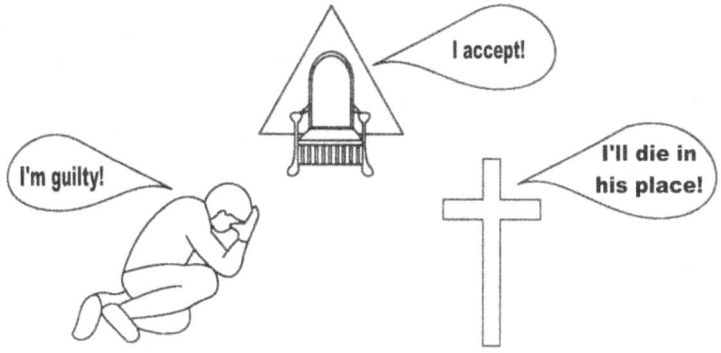

We all have a record of bad behavior. Jesus offers not only to erase the bad remarks from your book, but also to give you His own record, with many notes about His excellent behavior, in place of yours.

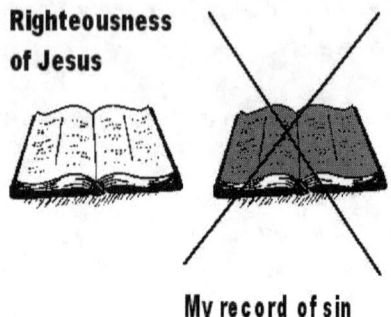

To illustrate this in financial terms, it's as if we had a debt of millions of dollars. Then Jesus not only pays the debt; He puts billions of dollars in our account!

Read Romans 9:30-32.

What was the Jews' error regarding righteous?

◊◊

Read Romans 11:6.

Some people think that you should combine faith and good works in order to be saved. They think that eternal life is partly given by grace and partly earned. According to this verse, do you think that this is correct?

◊◊

Read Romans 3:28.

According to this text, do good works contribute in any way towards our justification?

◊◊

You can either *give* somebody a car, or you can *sell* it, but you cannot do both at the same time! If you receive even a dollar for it, legally it is not a gift, but a sale. Eternal life is a gift and *cannot be sold*. We should not try to pay anything for it.

NOTE: In another lesson we will study the place of good works.

If someone is trusting any merit of his own for his salvation, he will never be sure if he has done enough. How good do you have to be to be saved? Really, the answer is that you would have to be *perfect*! But the problem is that *nobody is perfect!*

So how can you be saved?.... Only by faith in Jesus Christ!

Which of the following people understands what justification by faith means?

a. ____ "I think God will accept me into heaven because I have been a relatively good person, after all."

b. ____ "I think God will accept me into heaven because He is kind and will not be bothered by my sin."

c. ____ "I believe in Jesus, but I am not sure whether I have been good enough to deserve eternal life."

d. ____ "I know that I am a sinner, but Jesus died on the cross for me, and forgave me, so I know that I have eternal life."

e. ____ "You never know if you're justified until you die."

f. ____ "I am justified because I have been baptized."

JUSTIFICATION

1. The definition:

◊◊

2. The basis of our justification:

◊◊

3. The means of being justified:

◊◊

4. The result of being justified:

◊◊

FOR DISCUSSION

1. Have you received the gift of justification? If you haven't, you can do it now. Ask God for forgiveness for your sins: past, present and future. Read 1 John 1:9 and claim this promise!

2. Read Micah 7:18-19. What does God do with our sins, according to this passage? What does that mean?

TEXTS TO MEMORIZE

...Justified freely by his grace through the redemption
that is in Christ Jesus.

(Romans 3:24)

For we maintain that a man is justified by faith
apart from observing the law.

(Romans 3:28)

10
Sanctification

IT'S BOTH LEGAL AND PERSONAL

I have both a legal relationship and a personal relationship with my wife. We signed a document and publicly promised to take care of each other. We are legally responsible for our children. We even share financial responsibilities and are co-owners of our possessions. But there is more to our relationship than that! We also love each other! We enjoy talking, listening to music together, browsing in bookstores, watching TV, traveling, and sharing a good meal. I enjoy being with my wife!

It's the same with God; we have a legal relationship and a personal relationship. Before our spiritual conversion, we were legally guilty and deserving condemnation. We were separated from God and had no rights. Now we have been forgiven in a once-and-for-all legal way, which is called "justification," and we have become God's children with incredible "rights" of inheritance. However, we also need to develop our personal relationship with God. We need to learn to walk in a close relationship with Him and to grow in our character and our love for Him. This personal spiritual growth is what we call "sanctification."

The legal relationship will never change, but the personal relationship fluctuates, just like my relationship with my wife. When I offend her, it doesn't mean we need to get married again. However, it does mean that I need to ask forgiveness to remove the personal barrier and restore our sense of closeness. It's the same with God; when we sin, we do not lose our salvation, but we need to restore our personal relationship with Him.

How would you explain the meaning of these terms?

a. Sanctification
b. Libertinism.
c. Legalism.

BIBLE STUDY

There are two common errors regarding sanctification: libertinism and legalism. Libertinism means living without law, and legalism means living as a slave to the law. The libertine lives however he wants, without taking into account the will of God, and the legalist trusts the law and his own efforts to become righteous, instead of trusting the Lord. One doesn't care much about righteousness, and the other tries to make himself righteous.

We shall see in this lesson that both of these positions are errors. Sanctification is necessary because it is a part of our salvation, but the capacity to grow spiritually comes from God.

Read Romans 6:1-2.

After explaining that we are justified by faith in chapters 1-5 of Romans, Paul anticipates the question: If we are saved by grace, why not continue in sin?

What is his answer?

◊◊

Read Romans 6:14.

An important aspect of our salvation is liberation from the power of sin. Although we still sin, what can sin no longer do to us?

◊◊

Read 2 Corinthians 5:17.

When we believe in Christ, what do we become?

◊◊

What is your conclusion? Has a person really become a Christian if he doesn't care about pleasing God with his life?

◊◊

Which of the two common errors regarding sanctification is proved to be wrong by these passages in Romans and 2 Corinthians?

◊◊

Write the definition of libertinism:

◊◊

Read Galatians 3:1-3.

How did they receive the Holy Spirit?

◊◊

After becoming Christians, the Galatians were deceived by false teachers who insisted that they had to be circumcised to be saved. Paul wrote this letter to correct the error.

In verse 3, Paul says that if they are circumcised in order to be saved, they would be trying to obtain their goal by _____.

Read Galatians 5:2.

Explain Paul's point in this verse:

◊◊

Read Galatians 2:20.

How does Paul describe his new life?

◊◊

Read Galatians 5:22-23.

Write the different aspects of the fruit of the Spirit:

◊◊

Which of the two errors mentioned in the introduction is corrected by these passages in Galatians?

◊◊

DEFINITION:

SANCTIFICATION IS...

SPIRITUAL GROWTH

PUTTING SOME THOUGHTS TOGETHER:

Part of our problem with regard to sanctification is that often we exclude it from our concept of salvation. We emphasize justification as if it were the only aspect. For some, this can lead to licentiousness. Others may react to this and emphasize the importance of sanctification, but they make the mistake of taking their eyes off the Lord, trying to sanctify themselves, and they fall into legalism.

If we remember what *salvation* really means, it will help us avoid both errors:

Salvation is liberation from sin and all its consequences.

Obviously, this includes sanctification. It means that we must trust the Holy Spirit to grow spiritually.

A second part of our problem is that we tend to misunderstand what *faith* is. Sometimes we talk about faith as if it meant believing in the existence of God, or a merely intellectual acceptance of Christian doctrine. Obviously if someone "believes" only in this sense, he will not grow in his Christian life, because he never really became a Christian! He doesn't have a personal relationship with the Lord.

If we remember what *faith* really means, it will also help us to avoid both libertinism and legalism.

Faith is trusting Jesus as Lord and Savior.

This includes trusting Him to sanctify us.

Read Hebrews 12:1-2.

We should run the race with our eyes fixed on _____.

Jesus is the _____ and _____ of our faith.

This is the secret of the Christian life! Keep your eyes on Jesus! Justification is by faith in Him, and sanctification is also by faith in Him!

Which of these people is trusting the Lord for sanctification?

___ a. "I'm justified by faith, and now I can do as I please!"

___ b. "I'm justified by faith, and now I must prove I'm saved by being holy. god has done His part, and now I must do mine."

___ c. "I'm justified by faith and now I trust the Lord to help me grow."

___ d. "I believe in Jesus. In fact, I have a lot of faith. I must be saved, because everything is going so well with me in my career. God wouldn't bless me like that if I weren't saved."

___ e. "I believe in Jesus. He's the best man that ever lived. I'm going to live my life after His example."

___ f. "I believe in God. There must be a superior being who started the universe. All religions point to the same God."

REVIEW

DEFINE:

1. Libertinism:

2. Legalism:

3. Sanctification:

4. Salvation:

5. Saving faith:

FOR DISCUSSION

1. How can you detect if a person is making the mistake of libertinism? Of legalism?

2. Which error do you think is more common in your own life? In the Church?

3. Make a line drawing that represents your process of sanctification? Explain why you draw it that way.

TEXT TO MEMORIZE

Are you so foolish? After beginning with the Spirit, are you now trying to obtain your goal by human efforts?

(Galatians 3:3)

11
Faith and Good Works

How Do We Know if Our Bonsai is Alive?

My wife got a bonsai tree for Christmas one year, and we weren't quite sure how to take care of it. First, we understood that you should water it very lightly, so I sprinkled a few drops on it once in a while. To make the problem worse, the water seemed to roll off the pebbles to the side instead of filtering through the soil. By the end of two weeks, it seemed dead! All the leaves dried up and fell off. I finally called a store where they sold bonsai plants, and they explained that bonsais need just as much water as any other plant, and that I should drench it completely in order to revive it. So I put the whole thing under the faucet and soaked it. Then I took it outside to get some sun. I waited and waited for days, but still we saw no signs of life. I thought I had killed it, but Angelica encouraged me to be patient.

How would we know if our bonsai was alive? The only way to be sure was to wait and see if the leaves grew back. And sure enough, they did!

In a similar way, the leaves and the fruit in a person's life are evidence that he or she is spiritually alive. We all begin spiritually dead, but when the Holy Spirit gives us new life, there will eventually be evidence of that. For some people it may take longer than others, but it will come.

That's the secret to the relationship between faith and good works. Obviously, we don't produce fruit *so that* we can become alive. On the contrary, the leaves and the fruit come *as a result* of being alive.

1. What would you say to a person who said, "If salvation were by faith alone, there would be no motive for doing good works"?

2. Doesn't the Bible say we will be judged by our deeds? How can that be reconciled with the teaching that we are saved by faith?

BIBLE STUDY

We have already established that we are saved by faith, and that part of our salvation is sanctification. Still, there are some Bible passages that talk about being judged by our deeds, and that "faith without works is dead." How can these teachings be reconciled? Are they contradictions? Did the authors of the Bible have differences in their theology?

In this lesson, we will show how these teachings all fit together. They are not contradictions; each author emphasized different aspects of the same gospel.

Read James 2:14-26.

What does verse 26 say about faith without works?

◊◊

In this letter, James is correcting a misunderstanding of Paul's teaching about justification by faith. Some people were distorting this doctrine to excuse their libertinism. James explains that true faith leads to good works.

Read Ephesians 2:10.

What caused us to do good works?

◊◊

According to the previous lesson about sanctification, the source of our ability to do good works comes from God. In fact, He prepared them before we did them!

Read Matthew 25:31-46.

How can this passage be harmonized with others which teach that salvation is by faith? Actually, the explanation is simple: What is being taught here is that the good works are *evidence* that a person is saved, *evidence* that he has faith. Just as we studied in previous lessons, a person who has been born again experiences some changes is his life. The Holy Spirit begins to transform his sinful ways into a new lifestyle. If there are no such changes in his life, it only shows that he does not have true saving faith.

Good works are E _____ of true faith.

Read John 15:1-5.

If we don't bear fruit, what happens?

◊◊

What is the secret of bearing fruit? What must we do?

◊◊

Can a branch bear fruit if it is not connected to the vine?

◊◊

Thinking about this illustration in John 15, what do you think it means to "remain in Christ"?

◊◊

Just as a branch of a grape vine cannot bear fruit without receiving its nutrition (water and minerals) from the vine and its roots, so a Christian cannot bear fruit of good deeds if he is not receiving his strength from Jesus. This figure of the vine is another way of saying that we must trust Jesus, depend on Him, to be able to produce good works. Faith is our vital connection with Jesus.

Analyze this: Suppose a branch is broken, disconnected from the vine, lying on the ground,...

Could it bear grapes?

◊◊

What would it have to do to bear grapes?

◊◊

To be connected to the vine, or grafted to the vine, is a symbol of our spiritual relationship to Jesus.

◊◊

What do we need to be "grafted" into Jesus?

We need F_____.

Suppose a branch that is not connected to the vine wants to be considered part of the vine and therefore tries to bear grapes.

Is it possible?

◊◊

Wouldn't it seem ridiculous? Nevertheless, in a similar way, many people are trying to do the same thing spiritually! They think they can do good works to become a Christian. But this is exactly backwards! To be able to do good deeds, you need to become a Christian first! You need to be born again and put your trust in Jesus as Lord and Savior. Only then will you be able to bear fruit of righteousness.

CONCLUSIONS:

WITHOUT FAITH, THERE ARE NO TRUE GOOD WORKS.

WITHOUT GOOD WORKS, THERE IS NO TRUE FAITH.

GOOD WORKS ARE EVIDENCE OF TRUE FAITH.

WE DO NOT DO GOOD WORKS IN ORDER TO BE SAVED, BUT WE DO THEM BECAUSE WE ARE SAVED.

We say that without faith there are no *true* good works, because non-Christians can also do many things that seem very good, at least outwardly. The difference is, however, that their "good deeds" are not pleasing and acceptable to God because they do not come from faith, and because their internal motives are not correct.

Read Hebrews 11:6.

Without faith it is impossible to _____.

Think of a light bulb:

The light bulb itself is not the power that produces light; it's the electricity. But there will be no light if the tiny wire inside (the filament) is broken. If the filament is intact, the electricity passes through it and the light goes on. Therefore, the light is evidence that the filament is connected properly.

Think how this applies to spiritual life. Try to identify the parts of the illustration in the list below. From the following list of phrases, write the one in the space that corresponds: The Holy Spirit, The Christian, Faith, or Good works.

a. The light bulb	
b. The filament	
c. The electricity	
d. The light	

One more illustration: Imagine two kinds of trees, apple trees and orange trees.

Suppose that only apple trees could go to heaven. On judgment day, both kinds of trees come forward, mixed among themselves.

How could you tell the difference between an apple tree and an orange tree?

◊◊

Why does the apple tree produce apples?

◊◊

Can an orange tree produce apples?

◊◊

Applying this to spiritual life, the problem is that we are all born as "orange trees," so to speak. We cannot simply decide to produce apples, trying to earn our eternal life. On the contrary! We must be converted into apple trees first by faith, then we can produce apples. This requires nothing less than a miracle! God must change the very nature of the tree. Just as Jesus told Nicodemus, "You must be born again." This is the relation between faith and good works!

Identify the parts of the illustration in the left column below. Write each of the following phrases in the corresponding space: Christians, non-Christians, works without faith, true good works.

a. Apples	
b. Oranges	
c. Apple trees	
d. Orange trees	

REVIEW

1. Without faith, there are no real _____.

2. Without true good works, there is no true _____.

3. Good works are E _____ of true faith.

4. We can't do good works in order to be saved; we do good works_____.

FOR DISCUSSION

1. How can you tell the difference between Christians (the "apple trees") and non-Christians ("orange trees")? Is it always easy to tell by observing their lives?

2. How have you seen fruit in your life because of your relationship with Jesus?

Text to Memorize

Remain in me and I will remain in you. No branch can bear fruit by itself; it must remain in the vine. Neither can you bear fruit unless you remain in me.

(John 15:4)

12
Assurance of Salvation

HE HOLDS US TIGHTLY

A good father will hold his child tightly, especially when they are near something that could be dangerous, like the ocean or a busy street.

I remember when we visited the Grand Canyon with our young children. I don't think I ever had such a strong grip on them as when we were near the edge of the cliff, staring into the abyss!

God is our loving father who promises He will never let us go.

Since He takes the initiative in our salvation, we can be sure that a true believer never loses it. Our eternal life depends on Him, not on ourselves.

1. Are you sure that you're saved?

2. Are you sure you will never lose your salvation?

BIBLE STUDY

Some Christians live with the constant fear of losing their salvation. They are not experiencing the joy that could be theirs if they only understood the doctrine of eternal security. The Bible teaches that we already have eternal life and that we cannot lose it!

Read John 3:16.

What is necessary to obtain eternal life?

◊◊

Read John 5:24.

When do we obtain eternal life?

____ a. After we die

____ b. In the moment we believe in Jesus

____ c. After we are baptized

Read 1 John 5:12-13.

Do you need anything else besides Jesus to obtain eternal life?

◊◊

Read Romans 5:8-10 and Romans 8:1.

If God has already declared us "not guilty," would He go back on His word and condemn us?

◊◊

Paul's argument is that Christ died for us while we were sinners, therefore, what would he *not* do for us now that we have been reconciled with Him?

After explaining in the first seven chapters of Romans that we are justified and sanctified by faith, Paul crowns his doctrinal study with chapter 8 on eternal security.

◊◊

Read Romans 8:28-30.

Verses 29 and 30 have been called the "unbreakable chain." Some very important terms that we have been studying are linked together inseparably.

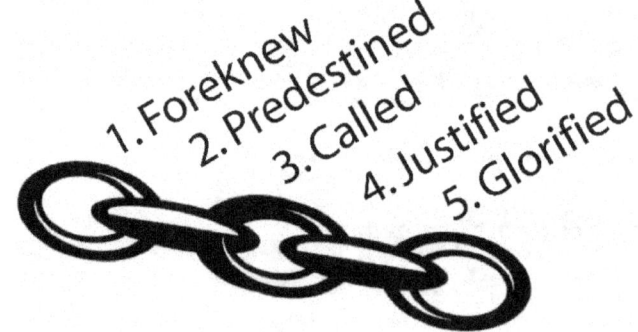

Those that God F _____, he also P _____.

Those he predestined, he also C _____.

Those he called, he also J _____.

Those he justified, he also G _____.

Let's review:

To *foreknow* us means to love us since before we were born.

To *predestine* us means to plan from beforehand that we would become like Jesus.

To *call* us means to have us hear the gospel and change our hearts so we can believe.

To *justify* us means to declare us righteous and not guilty.

The only term which we have not studied yet is *glorified*. It means that we will be transformed into the likeness of Jesus Himself. It is the last step in the process of sanctification. Of course, we do not become divine, with all His attributes and power, but we become like Jesus morally, sharing His holiness.

DEFINITION:

TO BE **GLORIFIED** MEANS...

TO BE MADE LIKE JESUS IN HIS HOLINESS

According to verse 29, what does God predestine us to be like?

◊◊

According to these verses, there is a group of people that go through the whole series of steps in their salvation. The same group of people who are foreknown and predestined are the same ones who are called, justified, and glorified. The chain is unbreakable. It makes sense: If God Himself predestines us to become conformed to the likeness of His Son, then He will carry out His purpose in us until the end.

The same people who are foreknown and predestined will be G_____.

The obvious question is, "How do I know if I'm one of those who have been predestined?"

The answer is simple: If you have *faith* in Jesus Christ, you know that you have been justified, and therefore that all the other things in the "unbreakable chain" happen to you, too.

Read Romans 8:31-34.

Explain the point of these verses in your own words:

◊◊

Read Romans 8:35-39.

Sum up in your own words the point Paul makes in these verses:

◊◊

What is your conclusion? Can someone who is saved lose his salvation?

Which of the following is true? Our salvation is sure because...

____ a. We have a lot of faith.

___ b. We no longer sin.

___ c. We have been baptized.

___ d. God is faithful to His promises.

___ e. We go to church every Sunday.

___ f. Our parents were Christians.

According to Romans 8:28, how many things does God work together for our good?

◊◊

This is one of the most comforting promises in the Bible! Stop and take the time to memorize this verse!

> And we know that in all things God works for the good of those that love him, who have been called according to his purpose.
>
> Romans 8:28

After memorizing it, write it:

This doesn't necessarily mean we will receive physical or material benefits; the emphasis is on spiritual benefits, making us more like Jesus. Try to think of ways in which God might work the following difficult experiences together for someone's benefit?

a. A broken leg.

◊◊

b. Losing his job.

◊◊

Also, this verse does not mean that we can sin and expect God to bless us for it!

When we sin, we don't lose our salvation, but it displeases God. It's like the relationship between a boy and his father. Let's suppose the boy lies to his father. He remains his son, but he has offended him, and he needs to ask forgiveness to restore the joy in their relationship.

When we sin, we are still God's children, but He is offended, and we need to ask forgiveness to renew our fellowship with Him. We have already been justified, and that *legal* relationship doesn't change, but the *personal* relationship needs to be restored.

Read John 13:10.

Being washed all over reminds us of our legal relationship with God. (We are justified.)

Washing the feet reminds us of our personal relationship with God. (We need to be forgiven repeatedly.)

Read John 10:27-30.

What does this passage teach about whether you can lose your salvation?

◊◊

Read Philippians 1:6.

What God has begun in us, He will _____.

REVIEW

1. Can a Christian have assurance that he is saved?

◊◊

2. Can you lose your salvation?

◊◊

3. Write the names of each link in the "unbreakable chain" of Romans 8:29-30:

4. Define "glorification":

◊◊

5. Write out Romans 8:28:

FOR DISCUSSION

1. If a person doesn't have assurance of salvation, does that mean he or she is not really a Christian?

2. What can you do if you begin to doubt your salvation?

3. What do you think about a person who seems to be a Christian, but falls away? Do you think he was really born again?

TEXT TO MEMORIZE

He who has the Son has life;
he who has not the Son of God does not have life.

(1 John 5:12)

13
Living by Grace

ARE YOU BURNED OUT?

David Seamonds tells of his experience as a missionary in India. A young man went to him for counseling, complaining of a sense of guilt, of anxiety, of anger, and of a low self-esteem. He was spiritually burned out. When he asked the young man the typical questions of whether he was reading his Bible, praying, and attending church, he found that he was doing better than the counselor himself in the practice of spiritual disciplines. He spent hours daily reading the Scriptures and praying, and he was attending many church activities. But something was not working. In that moment, Seamonds realized that the young man simply was not resting in the grace of God. He was trying to accomplish his own sanctification through his own human strength. Seamonds concluded that it was possible to do all the right things, without trusting the Lord, and this changed his whole ministry. After that, he began to put all his emphasis on the grace of God. (David Seamonds, *Healing Grace*. Wheaton: Victor Books, 1989).

It is very common that people begin their Christian life fully trusting Christ, then soon make the mistake of trying to sanctify themselves by their own strength. While it is true that we must fulfill our own responsibility, we can so easily fall into a dangerous trap, putting our attention on our own performance and taking our eyes off the Lord.

This is exactly what happened with the Galatians. They began well, but soon became legalistic, thinking that it was necessary to be circumcised and follow the Jewish customs in order to be saved. I believe that we are doing something similar when we pretend to "earn points" with God or obtain our own sanctification. Paul says in Galatians 3:3,

Are you so foolish? After beginning with the Spirit, are you now trying to attain your goal by human effort?

114

When I drive down the highway in my car, I need to observe the signs to arrive at my goal. However, if I fix my gaze only on the signs, and take my eyes off the road, I'll have an accident! The law in the Bible works that way; it's a sign pointing us to Christ, and we should not give so much attention to it that we take our eyes off Him. Sometimes our tendency is to prefer the law, even though it seems crazy. Why? Because of our pride; we want to feel like we can do something on our own.

I like to fix things around the house, but I have a problem; when something doesn't work, I usually just try harder. If a screw doesn't go in right, I just push harder and try to force it. Sometimes the screw pops out and falls on the floor. I may even cut my hand with the screwdriver. Brute force doesn't work very well. It's better to do it carefully.

A good golfer or baseball player knows that he can't simply hit the ball as hard as possible. He has to hit the ball squarely and direct it to the right place. The Christian life is like that; instead of just trying harder, we need to learn what it means to grow by GRACE. There are no simple formulas for spiritual growth, and we spend our lives learning more about it, but the key is to keep our eyes on Jesus, the author and perfecter of our faith.

Do God's blessings depend on how good I am?

BIBLE STUDY

Sometimes God's blessing is related to our obedience. If fact, some promises in the Scriptures are conditioned upon our faithfulness. (If we do such and such a thing, God will fulfill a certain promise.) However, in this lesson we want to warn of some possible distortions of this principle. We will show that God blesses us in spite of our imperfect obedience.

THE TRAP

Some people begin their Christian life trusting in God's grace, but then fall into some form of legalism, just as the Galatians. Remember: Satan is very astute, and he will do anything to keep us from trusting the Lord. Let's look at some ways in which we might mistakenly leave the pathway of grace.

First, remind yourself of the meaning of grace:

Grace is U _____ F _____ .

If we do not live by grace, we can fall into L _____, taking our eyes off the Lord.

Keeping this in mind, and remembering what we have studied in previous lessons, we will evaluate two mistaken attitudes, represented by persons "A" and "B."

A. PERSON "A" THINKS THAT WE WILL SUFFER IN THE SAME MEASURE THAT WE SIN.

He thinks that the more we sin, the more we will suffer. Like Job's "friends" (Job 4:7-8), he supposes that if we are suffering, it is because God is punishing us. He imagines God as a severe judge looking down from heaven, from behind the two tablets of the Ten Commandments!

ANSWER:

It's true that many times sin does have natural negative consequences (for example, if a young man uses drugs, it affects his health). Also, God sometimes disciplines us as a loving father, to help us grow (Hebrews 12:6-7). Nevertheless, God is not vengeful towards His children. He does not punish us in the sense of retributive justice. He forgives our sins and loves us in spite of our failures. He is a God of GRACE and MERCY. He is constantly working out all the events in our lives for our good.

Read Micah 7:18-19.

What does God do with our sins?

◊◊

Read Psalm 103:10-13.

Does God punish us as we deserve for our sins?

◊◊

God is like a F _____ who has C _____ on his children.

Read Hebrews 12:6-7.

Why does God sometimes discipline us?

◊◊

**GOD DOES NOT TREAT US AS WE <u>DESERVE</u> FOR OUR SINS,
BUT HE TREATS US ACCORDING TO HIS <u>GRACE.</u>**

It's very important to understand this so that we don't feel punished by God when something goes wrong in our lives. Some people, for example, feel that God is punishing them if they get sick or have financial problems.

Read Job 4:8 and 5:17.

Job's friend Eliphaz assumes that he knows why Job is suffering. What does he apparently think?

◊◊

Read Job 42:7.

What does God say to Eliphaz?

◊◊

Read John 9:1-3.

¿What can we learn about suffering from this incident?

◊◊

B. PERSON "B" THINKS THAT WE HAVE TO EARN GOD'S BLESSINGS.

This person turns the concept around. He thinks the more good works we do, the more blessings we receive. He says, "Maybe God does not *punish* us as we deserve for our sins, but He will not *bless* us if we are not doing enough good deeds. In other words, we must *earn* His blessings.

Some people try to make a deal with God. Maybe they begin to help needy people or give money to the church, expecting God to do some favor for them, such as healing a sickness or granting them financial prosperity.

Of course, it is good to help other people and be generous. However, this way of thinking also shows a misunderstanding of God's *grace*. We can't *earn* His blessings.

This doesn't mean that our behavior has no effect on our relationship with God. However, blessings don't depend on us, but on His loving kindness.

It's not hard to find illustrations of this in the Bible. All through the history of God's people we see that they have been unfaithful, but God blesses them anyway.

Read Hosea 14:4.

In this case, God scolds Israel for their idolatry, but continues to love them *freely*.

Read Luke 15:14-24.

How does the father in the story of the prodigal son show grace?

◊◊

What does this story teach us about God?

◊◊

This teaching about grace should never be taken to mean that it doesn't matter how we live. It's obviously important, and it affects our personal relationship with God. We can't abuse His grace and mercy.

Read Romans 6:1-4.

What misunderstanding does Paul warn us to avoid?

◊◊

The point we want to make is that God's blessing doesn't depend on US, but on HIM. Think of this: just how good would we have to be to somehow deserve God's love?

We clarify this point in order to highlight the main emphasis in all of these lessons:

THAT GOD BLESSES US BY PURE GRACE.

It's important to understand this in order to have correct motives for our obedience. If we think God only blesses to the extent that we obey Him we may try to *manipulate* Him. That is, we might obey Him to get something from Him.

Why should we obey Him, then? Simply because we *love* Him!

A true Christian really doesn't *want* to sin, because sin offends God. *He obeys out of love, not out of fear, or to gain something.* How would a man feel if his wife prepared a delicious meal for him, only to "butter him up" and ask him for a new dress!

Which of these people understands what it means to live by grace?

___ a. "God blesses me whenever He wants. It makes no difference whether I'm good or bad, so I guess I'll get drunk tonight!"

___ b. "I've failed the Lord several times this week. As a consequence, I'll probably have some kind of problem at work soon!"

___ c. "I would like for God to help me get into the university. I guess I'll have to start going to church for a while so He can answer my prayer."

___ d. "I'm praying for a job so I can provide for my family. I know I don't deserve it, because I haven't always been faithful to the Lord, but I trust He will be gracious to me."

___ e. "I've made a deal with God: if he heals my wife, I'll serve Him the rest of my life."

___ f. "I haven't had time to read the Bible lately, so I'm not even going to pray. It's no use. God won't hear me now."

THE SECRET:

> ### KEEP YOUR EYES ON JESUS.

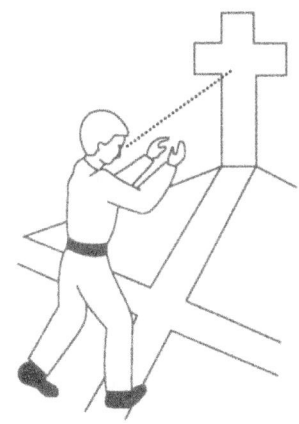

The secret of living by grace is always keeping your eyes on Jesus, not on yourself. Look to Him to see how you should live. Trust Him to receive the strength to do His will. Count on Him to shower His blessings upon you, not because you deserve them, but because He loves you.

Read Hebrews 12:1-2.

Run the race with all your strength, but with your eyes on Jesus, the author and _____ of your faith.

Read 2 Corinthians 9:8.

What makes us able to do good works?

◊◊

Read 2 Corinthians 12:9.

What does this tell us about God's grace?

◊◊

Read Ephesians 1:7.

What do the riches of God's grace provide for us?

◊◊

Read Acts 13:43.

What did Paul encourage them to do?

◊◊

Read Romans 1:17.

The NIV translation says: "For in the gospel a righteousness from God is revealed, a righteousness that is by faith from first to last, just as it is written: 'The righteous will live by faith.'"

Where does our righteousness come from?

◊◊

What do we need to receive it?

◊◊

Our life is like a bridge over a river, with strong foundations on each side made out of grace. We walk by faith all the way, from the beginning to the end.

Can you imagine someone trying to jump high enough to land on the moon? Wouldn't that be impossible? The only way to get to the moon is on a spaceship. In the same way, the only way we can get to heaven is through Jesus Christ.

The problem is that some people start out well, knowing that they are justified by faith in Christ, but then they somehow think they can continue on their own, and they take their eyes off Him. Can you imagine someone flying halfway to the moon in a space ship, then jumping out because he thinks he can make it the rest of the way in his own?

It's just as ridiculous to begin our Christian life by grace, then try to continue by human effort.

Read Galatians 3:3.

Paul says that it would be _____ to try to continue by human effort.

REVIEW

1. What is wrong with the idea that we suffer in direct proportion to our sin?

◊◊

2. What is wrong with the concept that we receive blessings in direct proportion to our obedience?

◊◊

3. We should obey God, not out of fear, or in order to gain something, but because _____.

4. The secret of living by grace is: _____.

FOR DISCUSSION

1. Discuss the errors represented by person "A" and person "B." Do you sometimes fall into the trap of thinking somewhat this way?

2. Discuss possible misunderstandings of the main point of this lesson.

TEXT TO MEMORIZE

...Let us run with perseverance the race marked out for us.
Let us fix our eyes on Jesus,
the author and perfecter of our faith....

(Hebrews 12:1b, 2a)

14
Why Do We Suffer?

BRUCE ALMIGHTY

In a popular movie, *Bruce Almighty*, the protagonist becomes angry with God for allowing him to have so many problems. God comes to him in the figure of a man and turns the city over to him for a while. Soon Bruce realizes that it is not so easy. He tries to answer everybody's prayers, but by doing this he ends up just causing problems. He lets everyone win the lottery, but the result is that the prize is divided among so many people that it's hardly worth anything and nobody is happy.

Sometimes we might feel like Bruce. But if we reflect briefly, we realize that we are too finite and limited to understand why God does things the way He does. We may not always be happy with how He manages things, but we need to learn to trust Him.

As they say, life is like a tapestry. We see the lose strings from below, and we can't quite make out the design. But God is weaving a beautiful picture that only He can discern from above.

FOR PREVIOUS REFLECTION

After studying about God's grace and love, an important question remains:

Why does God allow us to suffer? What do you think?

BIBLE STUDY

As we mentioned previously, some people think that when they suffer, it is because they have done something wrong, and God is punishing them. In this lesson, we will see that suffering for a Christian is not punishment, but a manifestation of God's grace for his good. We will study some of the different purposes in our suffering.

Read John 9:1-3.

Was the blind man being punished for some special sin he had committed?

◊◊

Read Job 1:1.

The story of Job is well known. His friends came to "comfort" him, telling him that his problems were due to some sin he must have committed, and that he should repent.

According to this verse, was Job suffering more than his friends because he was more sinful?

◊◊

CONCLUSION:

SUFFERING IS NOT NECESSARILY PUNISHMENT FOR SOME PARTICULAR SIN.

In one sense, as we studied in previous lessons, all suffering is a result of sin and the Fall. However, we can't relate every problem directly to some particular sin, and the amount of suffering does not necessarily reflect the amount of sin in a person's life.

SOME PURPOSES FOR OUR SUFFERING:

Read James 1:2-9.

According to this passage, what is one of the purposes of trials?

◊◊

Read Romans 5:3-4.

Suffering produces _____.

Perseverance produces _____.

Character produces _____.

Read 1 Peter 1:6-7.

What is the purpose of our trials, according to these verses?

◊◊

Read 1 Peter 4:12-13.

Why should we rejoice in our trials?

◊◊

Read Hebrews 12:4-8.

What is another reason for our suffering?

◊◊

If a father does not discipline his children, he doesn't love them!

Read 2 Corinthians 1:3-11.

What is another positive result of our suffering?

◊◊

Read Job 1:6-12.

Why did God permit Job to suffer?

◊◊

In Job's case, God permitted his tragedy and illness to show Satan that Job really loved the Lord. It was a test. The interesting thing is that Job never found out why he was suffering. If he had known, the test would not have been valid! The Lord only told him that there were many things he couldn't understand, indicating that he should *trust Him* and let *Him* control the situation.

Many times, God does not let us know exactly why we are suffering. The only thing He wants us to remember is that He loves us and He is working out everything for our good, even our suffering. *We* don't have to always know why, but *God* always knows why, and He has a good reason.

Read Romans 8:28.

Again, make sure you memorize this verse! Write it out in the box:

Read Genesis 50:20.

Joseph's brothers sold him as a slave. But even though he suffered, he became a leader in Egypt and was able to help his whole family survive a famine.

What is Joseph's attitude about what his brothers had done to him?

They intended _____, but God intended _____.

This is the key to how we should respond to suffering. There is both a negative side and a positive side. We shouldn't pretend that it isn't painful, but we should trust that God will use it for good.

Think about the cross: To crucify Jesus was the most horrible act in all of history. However, God planned His death to be the most wonderful thing that ever happened to us! His death brought us salvation! If God can use such an event for good, what can He not work together for good?

SUMMARY

SOME OF THE PURPOSES OF SUFFERING ARE:

a. To produce character.

b. To test our faith.

c. To allow us to share in Christ's sufferings.

d. To discipline us as God's children.

e. To enable us to comfort others that are suffering.

f. To test our love for God.

REVIEW

1. Write in your own words the six purposes of suffering mentioned in this lesson:

a.
b.
c.
d.
e.
f.

2. Can we always know the purpose of any particular experience of suffering?

◊◊

3. However, we do always know that God will work everything for our _____.

FOR DISCUSSION

1. Can you share an experience of how God turned something difficult in your life into something good?

2. Do you know someone you admire who has grown spiritually as a result of suffering? Tell a little about that person.

TEXTS TO MEMORIZE

Consider it pure joy, my brothers, whenever you face trials of many kinds, because you know that the testing of your faith develops perseverance. Perseverance must finish its work so that you may be mature and complete, not lacking anything.

(James 1:2-4)

You intended to harm me,
but God intended it for good
to accomplish what is now being done,
the saving of many lives.

(Genesis 50:20)

15
Review

Now What?

My wife Angelica and I had the opportunity to share these Bible studies with a friend once, meeting with her every week for several months. We carefully looked at every Bible passage, and she seemed to understand everything. We were so happy with the way she was responding. But when we came to the last lesson and I encouraged her to give her life to Christ, she just looked at me with a blank stare. I couldn't believe it! Her mind was understanding, but her heart was not responding.

The purpose of these lessons is to help you develop a personal relationship with Jesus Christ. If you "understand" everything in your mind, but don't respond to Him in your heart, it means little. You still need to personally come to Him, ask forgiveness, and ask Him to be your Lord. Turn your heart, your mind, and your life over to Him, and you will experience the joy of a new beginning!

The emphasis of the lessons has been on GRACE. Hopefully, you have come to understand GRACE better, and will experience greater joy and peace, responding to God's love with greater faithfulness.

These review questions will help remind you of the most important teachings of the booklet:

1. Define these terms:

a. Grace:

◊◊

b. Sacrifice of Atonement (Propitiation):

◊◊

c. Salvation (two definitions):

◊◊

d. The external call:

◊◊

e. The internal call:

◊◊

f. Repentance:

◊◊

g. Saving faith:

◊◊

h. Justification:

◊◊

i. Sanctification:

◊◊

j. Libertinism:

◊◊

k. Legalism:

◊◊

l. Glorification:

◊◊

2. God created everything in perfect H _____.

3. The Fall destroyed the relationships between:

a. People and _____,

b. People and _____,

c. People and _____, and

d. People and _____.

4. Write Romans 8:28:

5. Fill in the names of each link of the "unbreakable chain" of salvation in the proper order. (Romans 8:29,30).

6. Without faith, there are no true _____.

7. Without good works, there is no true _____.

8. Good works are E _____ of true faith.

9. We do not do good works in order to be saved, but we do them... _____.

10. We do good works, not out of fear, or to obtain something from God, but because we _____ God.

11. Can a Christian be sure of his salvation?

◊◊

12. Can a Christian lose his salvation?

◊◊

13. What is wrong with saying that we suffer to the same degree that we sin?

◊◊

14. What is wrong with saying that we receive blessings only to the same degree that we are obedient?

◊◊

15. Name six purposes of our suffering:

    a. _____

    b. _____

    c. _____

    d. _____

    e. _____

    f. _____

16. What is the secret to living by grace?

◊◊

Study the following drawing and talk about its meaning. How does it summarize the doctrines we have studied? See if you can use the drawing to explain the steps of our salvation process to someone else.

In eternity:
1. God loved me.
2. God predestined me.

In the future:
9. I will be glorified.

In my life:
3. God called me.
4. God regenerated me.

8. I am being sanctified.

5. I repented.

6. I believed in Jesus.
7. God justified me.

Answers to Review Questions

Lesson 1
1. Unmerited favor
2. Earning something by grace
3. So that nobody can boast

Lesson 2
1. Justice, mercy
2. All people are sinners.
3. Eternal condemnation
4. In Jesus' death on the cross, God shows both. He shows His justice by punishing sin in Jesus, and He shows His mercy by saving us.
5. A sacrifice which takes away the wrath of God

Lesson 3
1. Harmony
2. Good
3. Personal
4. Image
5. Similar to God, but not equal

Lesson 4
1. Independent
2. Arrogance
3.
    a. God
    b. Other people
    c. Nature
    d. Their own hearts

4. Through the sin of Adam, Sin and Death spread through the whole world.

Lesson 5
1. He died on the cross and rose again.
2.
    a. Reconciliation of all things in Christ
    b. Liberation from sin and all its consequences
3. Won, finished

Lesson 6
1.
    a. God causes us to hear the gospel.
    b. God brings us to Christ, renewing our hearts so that we believe in Him.
2. Before the foundation of the world
3.
    a. God's love
    b. Predestination
    c. The external call
    d. The internal call
4. To plan beforehand
5. Regeneration

Lesson 7
1. A change of attitude and a change of life
2. The first sense is when we first repent and become a Christian, like taking a complete bath, and the second sense is when we daily ask for forgiveness, like washing our feet (or some similar answer).

Lesson 8
1.
    a. Mere intellectual knowledge
    b. Faith in miracles
    c. An uncertain hope
2. Trusting Jesus as Lord and Savior

Lesson 9

1. A divine verdict saying we are righteous and not guilty
2. The work of Christ
3. Faith
4. Peace with God

Lesson 10

1. Living without law
2. Living as a slave to the law
3. Spiritual growth
4. Liberation from sin and all its consequences
5. Trusting Jesus as Lord and Savior

Lesson 11

1. Good works
2. Faith
3. Evidence
4. Because we are saved

Lesson 12

1. Yes
2. No
3. Foreknew, predestined, called, justified, glorified
4. Being made like Jesus in His holiness
5. "And we know that in all things God works for the good of those who love him, who have been called according to his purpose."

Lesson 13

1. God doesn't punish us as we deserve for our sin, but He deals with us according to His *grace* (or some similar answer).
2. God doesn't bless us because we deserve it, but because of His *grace* (or some similar answer).
3. We love Him
4. Keeping your eyes on Jesus

Lesson 14

1.
   a. To produce character
   b. To test our faith
   c. To allow us to share in Christ's sufferings
   d. To discipline us as God's children
   e. To enable us to comfort others that are suffering
   f. To test our love for God

Lesson 15

1.
   a. Unmerited favor
   b. A sacrifice which takes away the wrath of God
   c.
      (1) The reconciliation of all things in Christ
      (2) Liberation from sin and all its consequences
   d. God causes us to hear the gospel.
   e. God brings us to Christ, renewing our hearts so that we
      believe in Him.
   f. A change of heart and a change of life
   g. Trust in Jesus as Lord and Savior
   h. A divine verdict that we are not guilty
   i. Spiritual growth
   j. Living without law
   k. Living as a slave to the law
   l. Being made like Jesus in His holiness
2. Harmony
3.
   a. God
   b. Other people
   c. Nature
   d. Their own hearts
4.
   And we know that in all things God works for the good of those
   who love him, who have been called according to his purpose.
   Romans 8:28

5.

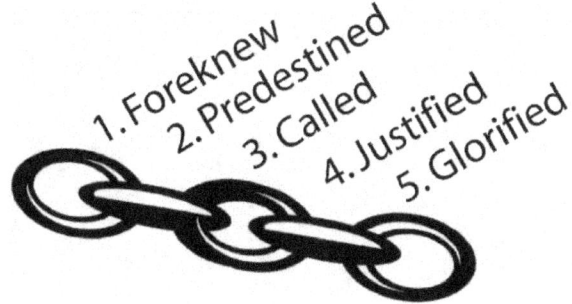

1. Foreknew
2. Predestined
3. Called
4. Justified
5. Glorified

6. Good deeds
7. Faith
8. Evidence
9. Because we are saved
10. Love
11. Yes
12. No
13. God does not deal with us according to what our sins deserve, but according to His GRACE.
14. God does not bless us because we deserve it, but by GRACE.
15.
    a. To produce character
    b. To test our faith
    c. To allow us to share in the sufferings of Christ
    d. To discipline us as God's children
    e. To help us comfort others
    f. To test our love for God
16. Keeping your eyes on Jesus

www.ingramcontent.com/pod-product-compliance
Lightning Source LLC
Chambersburg PA
CBHW060613130626
46555CB00002B/512